WHO WOULD WIN?

HAMMERHEAD

VS.

BULL SHARK

BY
JERRY PALLOTTA

ILLUSTRATED BY
ROB BOLSTER

Scholastic Inc.

New York   Toronto   London   Auckland
Sydney   Mexico City   New Delhi   Hong Kong

The publisher would like to thank the following for their
kind permission to use their photographs in this book:

Page 6: © Norbert Wu / Science Faction / Corbis; page 7: © Norbert Wu;
page 8: © Chris Newbert / Minden Pictures; page 9: © Visual & Written / SuperStock;
page 22: © Azure Computer & Photo Services / Animals Animals;
page 23: top: © Image Quest Marine; middle: © Seapics; bottom: © Brandon Cole

To cousin Jeanne Petronio, who comes from the hammerhead side of the family.
—*J.P.*

To Eddie.
—*R.B.*

ISBN 978-0-545-30170-1

Text copyright © 2011 by Jerry Pallotta.
Illustrations copyright © 2011 by Rob Bolster.
All rights reserved. Published by Scholastic Inc.
SCHOLASTIC and associated logos are trademarks and/or registered trademarks of
Scholastic Inc. WHO WOULD WIN? is a registered trademark of Jerry Pallotta.

26   15 16/0

Printed in the U.S.A.   40
First printing, September 2011

What would happen if a hammerhead shark came face-to-face with a bull shark? What if they were both the same size? What if they were both hungry? If they had a fight, who do you think would win?

GREAT HAMMERHEAD SHARK

Its head has a strange shape.

MAKO SHARK

The fastest-swimming shark!

> **REMEMBER THIS!**
> *Fish have gills, not lungs.*

MEGAMOUTH SHARK

A recently discovered deepwater shark with a huge mouth.

BULL SHARK

This shark has attacked more people
than any other shark.

WHALE SHARK

The largest fish in the world. It is a harmless filter feeder.

GREAT WHITE SHARK

The famous movie star
needs no introduction!

FACT
*Sharks are
saltwater fish.*

TIGER SHARK

The "garbage can" of the sea.
It eats almost everything.

Meet the great hammerhead. It can grow to be twenty feet long and can weigh one thousand pounds. Hammerhead sharks are easy to identify, because they have a head shaped like a hammer.

> **FUN FACT**
> *Scientists call the hammer-shaped head a cephalofoil.*

> **DID YOU KNOW?**
> *The largest hammerheads have a head that is three feet wide eyeball to eyeball.*

Hammerheads look scary, but they hardly ever attack humans.

SCIENTIFIC NAME OF BULL SHARK:
"Carcharhinus leucas"

Meet the bull shark. It got its name from its stocky shape and unpredictable behavior. It is an aggressive shark that lives in shallow water, preferring water less than one hundred feet deep. Female bull sharks grow to be twelve feet long and to weigh five hundred pounds.

INTERESTING FACT
Great white sharks often get blamed for bull shark attacks.

DID YOU KNOW?
Because they live in shallow waters, bull sharks are more dangerous to people than great white sharks or tiger sharks, which prefer deep waters.

Hammerheads hunt by themselves at night. During the day, they migrate in huge schools.

Bull sharks prefer to be alone.

BONUS FACT
Despite their solitary nature, bull sharks sometimes hunt in twos.

SHARK TRIVIA
The bull shark has many names: Zambezi shark, estuary shark, java shark, Fitzroy Creek shark, ground shark, Swan River whaler, cub shark, freshwater shark, and Lake Nicaragua shark.

TYPES OF HAMMERHEADS

FUN FACT
The funny-shaped head allows them to have more sensors. Hammerheads can smell better and sense fish better than other sharks.

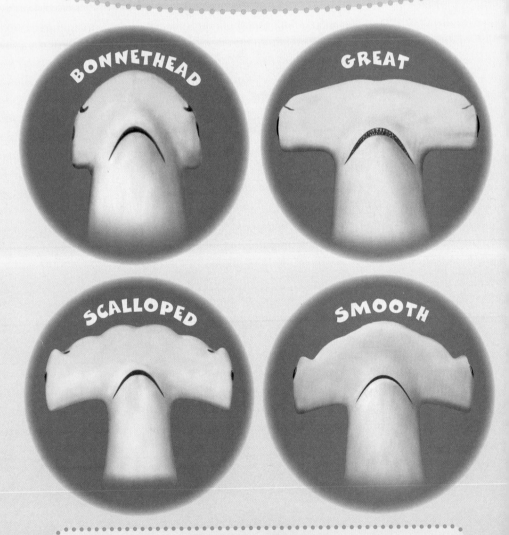

BONNETHEAD

GREAT

SCALLOPED

SMOOTH

DID YOU KNOW?
Some other hammerhead species are the scoophead, golden hammerhead, whitefin hammerhead, winghead shark, and scalloped bonnethead.

BULL SHARK
TRAVELS

Bull sharks swim in shallow coastal water. They often swim into estuaries and up freshwater rivers.

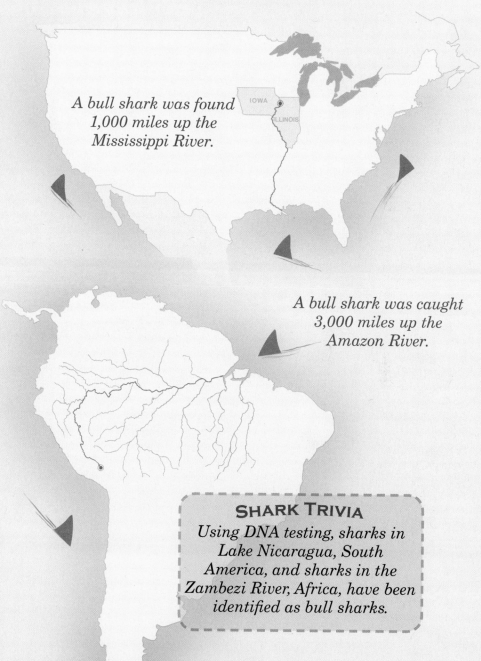

A bull shark was found 1,000 miles up the Mississippi River.

IOWA

ILLINOIS

A bull shark was caught 3,000 miles up the Amazon River.

SHARK TRIVIA
Using DNA testing, sharks in Lake Nicaragua, South America, and sharks in the Zambezi River, Africa, have been identified as bull sharks.

If you were scuba diving and a hammerhead swam at you, this is what it would look like.

If you were skin diving and a bull shark swam right at you, this is what you would see. Yikes!

FUN FACT

Bull sharks' heads are wider than they are long.

DID YOU KNOW?

Bull sharks are known for bumping their prey first. After the bump, they decide if they want to bite.

HAMMERHEAD TOOTH

Compared to other sharks, hammerheads have small mouths. But hammerheads, like all sharks, have scary-looking teeth!

TIGER SHARK

LEMON SHARK

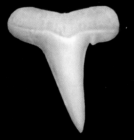

MAKO SHARK

NURSE SHARK

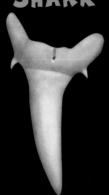

THRESHER SHARK

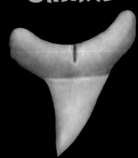

BLUE SHARK

BULL SHARK TOOTH

The bull shark has pointy bottom teeth and triangular top teeth. Its mouth is like a knife and fork. The bottom teeth hold the fish it catches, and the top jaw goes back and forth and cuts like a saw.

GREAT WHITE SHARK

GOBLIN SHARK

BLACKTIP SHARK

CROCODILE SHARK

WHALE SHARK

SAW SHARK

ANATOMY OF A HAMMERHEAD

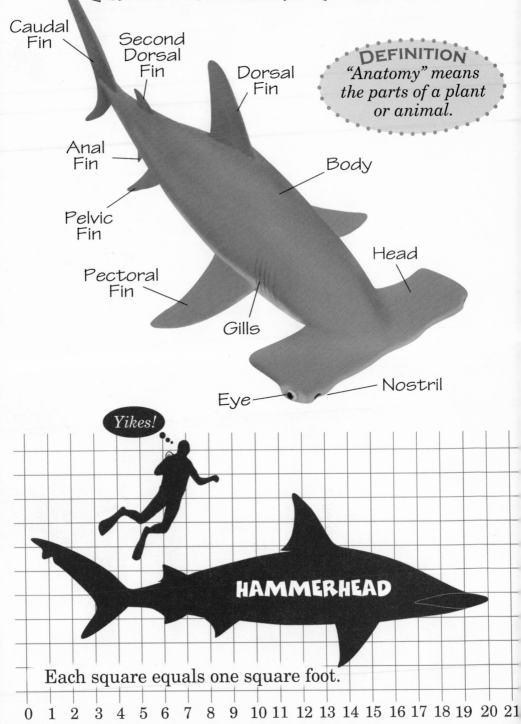

Caudal Fin

Second Dorsal Fin

Dorsal Fin

DEFINITION
"Anatomy" means the parts of a plant or animal.

Anal Fin

Body

Pelvic Fin

Head

Pectoral Fin

Gills

Eye

Nostril

Yikes!

HAMMERHEAD

Each square equals one square foot.

0 1 2 3 4 5 6 7 8 9 10 11 12 13 14 15 16 17 18 19 20 21

ANATOMY OF A BULL SHARK

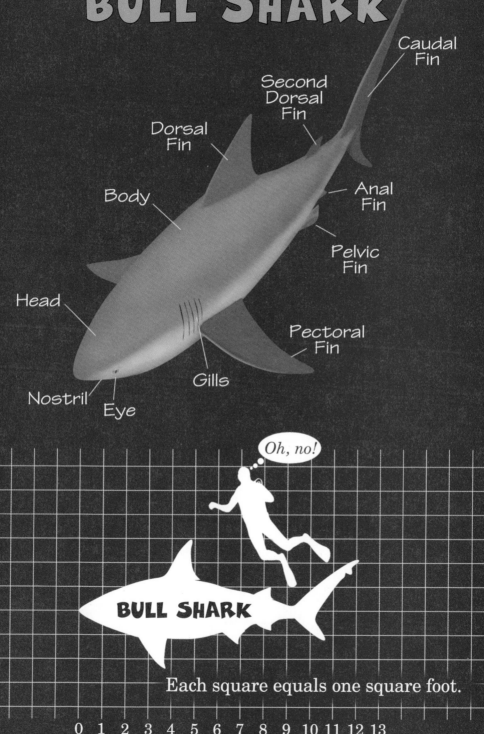

Caudal Fin

Second Dorsal Fin

Dorsal Fin

Anal Fin

Body

Pelvic Fin

Pectoral Fin

Head

Gills

Nostril

Eye

Oh, no!

BULL SHARK

Each square equals one square foot.

0 1 2 3 4 5 6 7 8 9 10 11 12 13

When engineers design aircraft, sometimes all they have to do is look at nature.

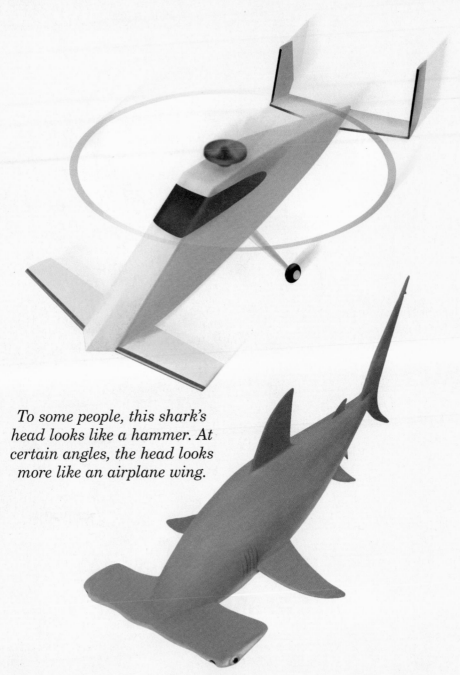

To some people, this shark's head looks like a hammer. At certain angles, the head looks more like an airplane wing.

The wing-shaped head gives the shark stability when it is swimming.

You could say that the space shuttle was designed by nature millions of years ago.

Look at the shape and design of the bull shark.

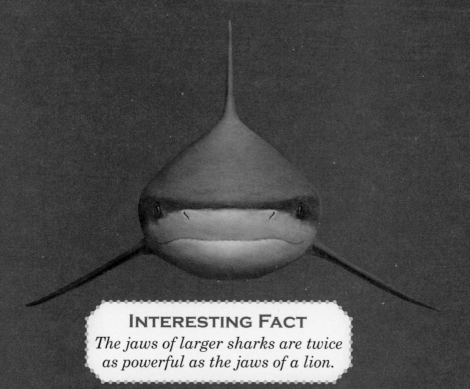

SHARK

The great hammerhead and the bull shark are different sharks, but their tails are similar. Take a look!

GREAT HAMMERHEAD SHARK

WHALE SHARK

NURSE SHARK

COOKIECUTTER SHARK

FUN FACT

A ragged-tooth shark can touch its tail with its nose.

BONUS FACT

A tail fin is also called a caudal fin.

20

TAILS

A shark uses its tail to propel itself forward. It steers with its tail and its side fins.

BULL SHARK

BONUS FACT
Almost all sharks have a vertical tail.

THRESHER SHARK

BLACKTIP REEF SHARK

TIGER SHARK

SHARK FRIENDS

Sharks and pilot fish are friends.

For example, pilot fish eat parasites off the shark's skin. Pilot fish get to eat the shark's leftover food scraps. And pilot fish stay safe from predators by swimming with the shark.

TOUGH FACT
*Sharks have rough skin—
it is like armor. They have teeth on
their skin called denticles.*

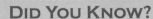

DID YOU KNOW?
*Cleaner wrasses are fish that clean
sharks' skin. Some even go in the
sharks' mouths.*

SHARK HITCHHIKERS

Remoras are fish that hitch a ride on the shark. Remoras have a suction disc and attach themselves.

SHARK TRIVIA
Remoras are also called sharksuckers.

This is a remora.

ICKY FACT
Some parasitic copepods and worms attach themselves to sharks.

THINGS A
HAMMERHEAD SHARK
CAN'T DO

They can't
parachute.

They can't
sing like Elvis.

They can't ride a
bicycle.

THINGS A
BULL SHARK
CAN'T DO

They can't yo-yo.

They can't paint
like Michelangelo.

They can't bake
cupcakes.

A giant hammerhead is cruising along. A bull shark is looking for food.

INTERESTING FACT

A hammerhead uses its wide head to detect and pin stingrays to the ocean floor. They are its favorite food.

The hammerhead sees the bull shark, but is not interested. Huge sharks are not his type of food. The hammerhead looks for something smaller and easier to eat.

DID YOU KNOW?

The ferocious bull shark easily adapts to captivity and living in an aquarium.

The bull shark feels threatened and is not afraid to pick a fight. He swims right at the hammerhead.

The bull shark opens its mouth and tries to ram the hammerhead. The hammerhead's better eyesight allows him to turn and avoid the bull shark. The hammerhead dodges away.

The bull shark is angry and darts at the hammerhead again. The hammerhead ducks. Both sharks are excellent swimmers.

The bull shark attacks again. This time it bites the hammerhead's tail. The hammerhead turns to defend itself. But the bull shark catches a piece of the hammerhead's tail and rips off a chunk.

The hammerhead is bleeding and can't swim as fast. His blood excites the bull shark even more. At full speed, the bull shark rams the hammerhead and knocks him off balance. The bull shark bites the hammerhead a few more times.

The hammerhead is defeated. The bull shark will eat him. Other sharks in the area can smell the meal.

The bull shark won today. Maybe the next time these two species meet, the hammerhead will recognize the danger right away.

WHO HAS THE ADVANTAGE?
CHECKLIST

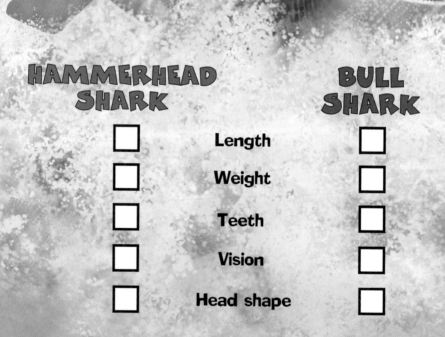

HAMMERHEAD SHARK		BULL SHARK
☐	Length	☐
☐	Weight	☐
☐	Teeth	☐
☐	Vision	☐
☐	Head shape	☐

Author note: This is one way the fight might have ended. How would you write the ending?